DEDICATIONS

I dedicate this book to God, my children, my family, and friends who have prayed with me, and for me, over the years Tawnya Lynn and Hollie Dawn, thank you for the encouragement and gentle pushes along this journey.

To those who may pick up this book and give me the chance to share what happened to me. I pray this brings you closer to Jesus.

Chapter 1

You might be asking yourself why you picked up this book out of all the books available on the shelf. Why would you want to read my life story? How is my story different from any other story previously told? Well to begin with, it is my story, so I know it's true! Maybe, It's because we can all relate to trying to find our own identity; like having an identity given to you or feeling as though you have been labeled with an identity you didn't ask for. I have been told "God has a plan for you" and "after everything, that happened to you, after all you've been through, it had to happen for a reason." No pressure, right?! I've been told by so many that the world needs to hear my story! However, what most people don't know about me is, I'm a great big chicken! I am terrified of public speaking. Now, if you're standing in line at Subway near me or I encounter you over the phone, you're about to hear all about my time with Jesus and what happened to me! Maybe you've already heard some of my story and that's why you grabbed this book, but I pray God uses these words to help you heal, find him, and solidify who you are in Christ and how amazing Jesus is! I have been labeled by many as "the coma girl." Once you hear my full story, you will understand why there could be a worse label I could be stuck with.

Chapter 2

In a world where we can identify as anything, and people sure choose freely. "Hey, I'm an attack helicopter" was an example given by my daughter during a youth question and answer session. But really, who is going to question you nowadays? Could I, or you, really identify as "November Female Unknown"? Have you ever felt unknown, unseen, or even unwanted? I grew up a simple country girl in a ridiculously small town. I could not wait to get off my grandfather's farm. I remember telling my grandfather remarkable stories of the adventures that I would find. He used to always say to me "you'll spend all your time trying to leave this farm and once you do, you'll spend a lifetime trying to get back to these simple days." Funny how those words have a different meaning once you grow up. As we go through life, we grow into our own identities. We are influenced by who we choose to look up to, whether those people are family members, movie stars, or sports figures. I remember when I was growing up, teachers would often ask us what we wanted to be. Many were hoping to find that their identities would lead them to being a doctor, lawyer, or even a princess. Some wanted to be the next president of the United States, an astronaut, or a teacher. Our identities are often built from things that happen to us from childhood through adulthood. Whether that be our upbringing, our cultural influences, or even a tragic event that takes place. These moments, influences or events place an identity on you like "the coma girl". In a world so full of deceit, how do we find who we truly are? Why do we most often receive our labels from our most tragic events?

Chapter 3

I could have spent my whole life labeled as an abused child. I could have held on to that identity forever. As a young girl, I was left in the care of someone that should have protected me, but he did not. My innocence was stolen and my world as I knew it would never be the same. I could have remained his victim forever. Although perhaps, in some ways I have. What happened to me was nothing short of horrifying and life altering, but I didn't want that to be my life label nor my only identity. I refused to allow him to win or have that kind of power over my entire life. I knew I had to push forward. I was raised in church, even though growing up I really didn't want to go. I was read bible stories, taught lessons, and attended youth groups regularly. I knew of God but did not know Him. I was familiar with some of his stories but didn't really think about God much at all. When my grandfather passed away, my relationship with God further diminished. The first chance I got; I was gone from that small town. I was off to build a much grander life, or so I thought, and that's when I met "the best guy ever." I'm sure you've heard a girl say that a time or two, huh? You quite possibly have been the girl who uttered this phrase yourself a time or two. This man had everything, and by "everything" I mean his life was so different from the life I'd lived thus far. He was kind, had money, fast cars, and the best bonus was his amazing parents. I truly enjoyed my time with his mom. To this day I hold close to my heart, and treasure, many of my memories with her. He was fun to be around and just plain funny. He made me laugh often, until he wasn't funny anymore and the "honeymoon phase" was over. He had separated me from everyone and everything I knew. He convinced me to move to a completely different country where I was alone and primarily dependent on him.

Chapter 4

In that whole new country, I was identified as the "American girl with a silly accent". His pattern of being loving, kind, making myself worth soar, or like he was proud to have me was an ever revolving door, then it vanished in an instant. Everything he said suddenly had a double meaning. No matter which way I would interpret what was said, he would twist it, so I felt dumb. I believe he was hoping I would start to view myself as a failure. You might ask, how could someone give one person that much authority over their life? Apparently, it happens one small step at a time. My heart was shattered time and time again. I would believe all was going to okay, but then the pattern would repeat itself once more. I had set out to achieve what I thought was a simple dream, the American dream. I wanted to have that perfect family. Marry a man who would be the perfect daddy and I would be the perfect mama. We would have the perfect house with that white fence and with perfect babies. Maybe we would even have a dog! I fought hard to make that dream a reality. I wanted so badly to identify us as that perfect family, from my dream, but ultimately that was never going to happen.

Chapter 5

Fast forward some time, and I found myself identifying with yet another type of identity. I was sitting in a women's shelter, not the first or second time, but multiple times, and I felt like I now carried another label. I had my small girls with me; one at my feet and the other by my side. I distinctly remember, in one of the shelters a woman said to me, "I know exactly how you feel". I asked her if she was also in an abusive situation, she informed me that she was not. I thought to myself, "how could she comprehend what I was going through or understand how I was feeling"? I do not remember her name, but she left quite an impression in my mind with what she said to me next. "How you're being treated and allowing yourself to be treated, is teaching your daughters exactly how they should also be treated." These were, and still are, incredibly heavy words that have remained with me throughout the years. But I was stuck in that cycle of the "honeymoon phase" and lie that "this time it would be different". I was lost. I wanted my girls to have a family that was together forever. I kept saying to myself, "if I only did better", "if only I tried harder". I wish the picture they would forever have painted in their minds would have been one of a perfect family. Instead, they will live with the image of an abused mom and broken family. I wanted better for them. I wanted my girls to identify with and build their lives from the perfect family they grew up in. That perfect family never happened, but it didn't matter because I had to make the best choice for my beautiful girls. We left. We eventually ended up in Colorado with a better plan; or so I thought.

Chapter 6

I was prepared to begin building a stronger version of myself in my life. I discovered and grew deep in the pagan religion. I completely turned away from God. My birth father had told me numerous stories over the years, and I was determined to seek those roots. I wanted to identify as a pagan. I began working towards a high priestess status. I dove deep into studying, learning, and fully practicing the customs and beliefs. I wanted to build a family as a strong pagan priestess with beautiful priestess daughters. I had gained a large following and my waiting list for card reading was extraordinary. Our group even had its own radio talk show. During this time in my life, I met a new man. I thought he would be a good father figure. After all, he was a police officer in the military so I was immediately convinced there would be no worry for abuse in our relationship. The thing about everyone's own identity is you can't force someone to be what you want them to be; and we shouldn't!
I wanted him to identify as a hardworking man and father. He wanted to identify as

an alcoholic who was fully dependent upon pills. I can still hear the echoes of my ex-husband playing in my mind. "You'll never make it without me" and "you're such a gullible, naive girl". Immediately, I set out to prove to him just how wrong he was. I started a new job at this cute little kiosk. I worked that job and became a manager there in a short amount of time. When given the chance, I bought that cute little kiosk and began my journey as a business owner. I thought to myself, "Ha! I showed him! Telling me, I couldn't do it without him". I believed at that point my children would be able to identify our little family as strong and proud. They now had a mother who was successful pagan high priestess, a business owner our little family was growing we was able to take in children who needed extra love. It's intriguing to think how many identities one person takes on in their life. I no longer was that little girl who was abused and forgotten, unworthy of love, or a battered wife. I was no longer a woman who was made to feel not good enough because I gained too much weight due to pregnancies, failed at tasks, or said the wrong things at the wrong times. I was now stronger, and things were better. Being around somebody that identified as a drinker depleted not only my bank account, but also my mental account. I had to make changes, big changes once again. That I knew for certain.

Chapter 7

I had lost everything. I took my babies, my dog, everything we could fit into my Dodge Magnum and headed across the US. I was on my way back to the very place I was so desperate to leave all those years ago. At this point, I was homeless. I made the decision to return to the home where I grew up with the most loving grandparents who had old school values and true love in their hearts. Their kind of love was the type of love I always prayed to find one day. Much to my surprise, home wasn't quite like I remembered it. Both myself, and my girls, were made to feel like outcasts, unwanted and unwelcome. We were in the very home my grandfather promised me would always be my haven. I had no choice but to leave that home. We were blessed enough to be offered a small space in a relative's attic. It was small, but we were safe. I made the mistake of talking with my ex and bought all the lies he had to tell. I was a completely different woman now, so why wouldn't I assume he was a completely different man. I kept telling myself "It'll be better this time". I was going to be stronger and refused to allow our old pattern of living to happen and repeat itself. I sold myself the lie that maybe everything that had happened before had to happen for us to have the perfect family image the second time around. Maybe we really were going to be the family that beat the odds and would spend time together forever. At this point, anything seemed better than being where we were. The honeymoon phase came and went faster than expected. I quickly found out our life was not going to be different. Not even the slightest bit. But how? I was stronger, and how did he not see my worth now? How could he not value the woman who was standing in front of him? I thought he would see that he could not walk all over me now. I was back in his country of all places and here he was still the precise person he was when we left all those years before. I still owned my business at this point, and I was doing everything I could to make it work, but things were falling apart quickly. Apparently, I tried to identify as someone better than I was; at least that is how I felt. I sank into a deep depression. I wanted to make a perfect life for my children, and I kept failing horribly. By this point I was beginning to label myself as a worthless failure, terrible mother, and really didn't know why I was even still here. In that time was thinking was I really that unworthy of love and affection? Was I really a mother who could not make her children proud? No matter how much effort I put in and how hard I tried, I just kept failing.

Chapter 8

I ended up in Florida with a friend of mine, who I don't remember the name of. We'll get to that later, though, but let's just say there is a great place in Florida where you can bring your business and children, and everything seems to be successful.

This is where my memories begin getting choppy and go blank.

I don't remember coming to Florida. I don't recall much from this point in my life forward. I don't know what my identity was or who I was trying to be within myself. Why didn't I do to better myself along the way? How were all those memories completely lost? It was all just gone. One memory that is eternally burned into my memory is a phone call I received. It was the worst kind of call a mama can get. Someone on the other end of the line told me my son took his own life. I remember the shadows on the walls and the look on my daughter's face. I vividly remember the immediate sick feeling in my stomach and heart. That feeling of receiving the worst news I had ever heard and holding it back for just a few seconds before I knew life would forever change after that moment. I didn't want to have to deliver the saddest news my heart had ever gotten to my girls. I had to sit down and tell my little girls that their brother was gone. And the identity I certainly never wanted them, or myself, to have had now been given to us. We were now the family of a suicide victim. There was nothing in this world that could stop the pain that I was feeling. I don't know how long I had been in Florida or where exactly I was even living. All that stands out from that moment in my life is that loss. I cannot tell you who I was at that moment, let alone tell you the role model I was being for my daughters. Our family forever changed on that day, April 1, and suicide robbed us of a sweet young man who was an incredible part of our family. My sweet boy fought his depression for many years, and I was told he was a very strong person but simply couldn't be strong anymore. I've been asked numerous times, "How does someone move on from that?" My only answer, one day, and sometimes one breath at a time. That's how.

Even in my blank spaces that are still missing today. I'll hear a song or have an emotion, too, but not a memory that fits it. Talk about a strange feeling. I suppose we must fast forward a bit to understand what I'm talking about, and to do that, we will start with my very first memory as "November Female Unknown." Why has abuse been a large part of my life story? What was the identity of the person I was supposed to be? This is the part of the story when things start to get tricky. Even in my "blank spaces", that are still missing to this very day, I'll hear a song or feel a specific emotion and not have a memory associated with it. Let me tell you what a strange feeling that is! Let's fast forward a bit so you can understand exactly what I'm talking about. To do that we have to go back to my first memory as "November Unknown". I woke up to the sound of a machine, beep... beep.. beep, and another weird sound. I opened my eyes and saw a beautiful woman with the most breath taking blue/green eyes I'd ever seen. She said, "Mom, it's me!" My initial thought was, "Who is she calling Mom?" and "I have a child?" My next thought was "wow, this beautiful woman called me Mom!" Before I comprehended what I was doing, I stood up. I needed to go to the washroom, and without any warning I hit the floor! No one tells you when you wake up from a coma that your body doesn't exactly function as it should. My legs were so atrophied that they could not support me. Before I get ahead of myself and completely lose you in the process. I died! Yes, I died and was revived, then woke up in the hospital from a coma. Which brings me to the November Unknown" identity part of my life.

Chapter 9

On September 13th, 2022, I apparently came down with covid. I was terribly sick and could barely walk. The man that I was supposed to marry, I'll explain that in a moment, had put something in my food and/or drinks. I'm not truthfully sure what his true intention were, but I was told he was trying to "put me out of my misery". A call was made to 911. The man who did this, a man I was supposed to have married. Thankfully, due to covid shutting everything down we had never taken that walk down the aisle. I don't remember meeting him, dating him, or wanting to be married to him. I do not remember wanting to be a bride, let alone being told that my wedding was canceled. What a devastating thing to hear, your wedding was canceled because the world shut down. Or at least you would think it would be devastating, I honestly didn't seem to be affected. I'm sure that was a tragic, and sad, moment in my life. In hindsight, it is absolutely a lesson learned. We must remember to thank God for unanswered prayers. When EMS showed up, I was face down and unresponsive to pain. The report states they wrapped me in a sheet and took me out of my home. The EMS worker, thankfully, saw my chest slightly move up and down, so they rushed me to the hospital; leaving without any documentation of who I was. I was registered at the hospital as November Female Unknown, just another Jane Doe. It didn't matter in that moment if I was a victim of childhood and adulthood abuse, an almost bride, a mother, a parent who lost her son to suicide, or a homeless woman. I later went and got the reports from that day. I felt the need to know and hopefully have the missing parts of what happened to me filled in since I couldn't remember anything at all

Chapter 10

I laid in that hospital bed, as November Female Unknown, with a 4% chance of survival. Praise the Lord, he knew my name the entire time. Let me pause here to answer a couple questions that I was asked hundreds of times regarding my time in the coma. "Did you hear people talking to you?" "Could you hear people moving around the room?" The answer to both questions is no. I could not hear anything that was said to me, about me, or what the EMS, nurses, or doctors were doing to me. I also did not hear the prayers of a man who came into my room, put oils on me, and covered me in his prayers; then laid a cross next to me. Pausing here for a little back story. This man, and his wife, came into my life when I was feeling forgotten and completely alone. I was feeling like there was nowhere and no one for me to turn to, I reached out to God saying, "Fine God, if you're real I'm yelling for you!" I started driving and ended up in a church parking lot, and might I add not even the closest one to where I was. I pulled into that church, and as I as sat in my truck crying, and emptying my heart and soul over to God. I noticed pastor and church leader had come walking out. This couple has since then told me that the moment he saw me the Holy Spirit told him, and his wife, I was going home with them. To this day, they have become my Mama Peggy and Grandpa Larry. This man and woman hold an eternally special place in my heart. The man who came in and had prayed over me was one of the church leaders who had helped me when I was at my lowest. I'm telling you this, because where I was, none of it happened. Where I was and what I was doing was racing down some of the most intense raging river rapids on a boat! I was on this boat with Jesus himself! When I looked at this man, in less time than it takes you to take in a breath, I knew who he was. Let me tell you though, he looks nothing like any photo we have ever seen, or any picture ever painted. And yes, I have searched to find a depiction of him that matches who I saw. When was sitting in my truck, crying, and emptying my heart and soul over to God.

Chapter 11

It may sound silly, or even ridiculous, but there is no way for me to explain his image. What I can tell you is Jesus is every feeling you have ever felt, all at one time. Jesus is a magnificent man. He is powerful, strong, firm, loving, gentle, and kind yet firm and strict. He is perfect, in every literal sense of the word. If you sat down and thought of the most perfect love you've experienced, He is greater. To try and put it in some kind of human perspective, think of how scary it would be to have your child go missing and suddenly have them returned to you. Imagine the overwhelming feeling of love and excitement mixed with fear and relief. Or maybe you've had the most amazing father figure and the feeling that his embrace gives you in moments of fear, heartbreak, or love, His is greater. Although, if I am being honest, I don't even know if those feelings explain His love. Jesus is everything you would ever want a father to be to his children. As I write these words, I can recall every detail of him. I am usually in tears when I think about the memories I have of my time with him. I highly value these memories since I am missing so many of my life before. I feel Jesus and remember him so vividly. I also remember the water we were in being so powerful, but crisp. If you've ever had the chance to stand next to Niagara Falls, on the Canadian side, close to where the falls roar over and crash down to the bottom, that's the kind of power I felt. I remember the waves breaking and roaring down the sides of the boat. I remember there was a rope, and I had grabbed onto it. I remember saying, "oh no, I'm scared" but not actually feeling fear. I said it because I knew it was something I probably would have said in that moment, while in full blown tears and screaming. Jesus though, he was unbelievably calm and unmoved by the raging waters. He was within my reach the entire time, but I never reached for him. I never touched him, not once.

Chapter 12

I do have to tell you I connect with songs on a deep level. I always have. I'm sure you've heard of the song "I Can only Imagine" by MercyMe. We can all identify with the message this song delivers. Only I don't find myself needing to imagine anymore. I was in his presence, but I didn't touch him. I cannot tell you why I didn't touch him, I just know that I did not. I do know that the next time I am in his presence I will leap into his arms. Just standing in His presence made me feel known and that for the first time ever in my life I knew I was enough. I knew that he was proud of me, loved me, and He fully accepted me for precisely who I was. I knew I had never failed him. I was, and now and forever, His. He said to me, in a firm and strict fatherly loving voice but with a deepness to it, "Move when I say move, and stay when I say stay and you will be okay." How utterly simple is that message? Why do we complicate His directions? I remember when He spoke those words to me, it was like a weight was instantly lifted from me. I was forever changed in that moment. Looking back, I know that God put me in my most fearful situation to show me that He was and always has been in complete control over my life. How simple would our lives be if we were to simply follow Christ's directive. What if we would move when He tells us to move, and stay when He tells us to stay? What if we were to remain patient and allow God to guide us. How magnificent would our lives be and how differently would we view ourselves?

Chapter 13

Are you labeled with an identity today that you aren't in agreement with or happy with. Maybe you are utterly lost in the confusion of who you are supposed to be because of something that was done to you or a tragic event that happened to place an identity on you. If you are willing to focus your sight on Jesus and set your heart to hear what He is saying to you and what He wants from you, I promise you will find your truest identity through Him. I find myself seeing how us losing our sight and faith in Jesus is like the way Simon Peter did when he dropped his eyes while walking on the water toward Jesus; and began to sink. My time spent with Jesus went by differently than my time in a coma. That 4% label chance of survival didn't matter to Him. He was in charge and knew that I was going to wake up against all odds set forth by the medical professionals. I remember seeing the face of the woman who called me, Mom, and falling to the floor. Next thing I knew I was standing in the washroom without a mirror, but I could see my reflection in the towel dispenser hanging on the wall. I didn't recognize the face looking back at me. I had never seen her before in my life. I remember thinking "who is this?" but I knew I needed to call my job to report off work. I guess that was my trained human brain or simple basic human instinct. How incredible are our minds? I didn't know my own child, or recognize myself, but instinctively knew how to call Ms. Susan, my supervisor. By the way she is an amazing supervisor and woman. She held my job for me through everything. Ms. Susan and a woman named Brittany helped me rebuild my lost confidence. I might have spent time with Jesus, but I did not feel mentally strong while fighting to regain my memories or trying to remember all the things I needed too. I had to re-learn how to walk as well as re-learn my day-to-day living, along with all that I needed to know pertaining to my job. I overloaded myself with questions like, "How am expected to just pick up where I left off?" Having women like Ms. Susan, Brittany, and Elizabeth, who were patient with me, answered all my questions, but most importantly empowered me to boost my self-confidence can never be properly repaid or thanked. They helped me to keep my job and make sure I was still good at it. You ladies are amazing! Having women like you my corner was and forever will be a blessing.

Chapter 14

During my time with Jesus, we spoke about men, women, and how he created Men and women with a specific yet different from each other purpose in mind. Maybe that is a story for another day, but praise God I woke up in that strange hospital. My next memory from when I awoke, was being in a room with large windows and two women were standing in front of a large window. One was my biological mother, and the other was Mama Peggy. They were together, what a strange sight that was. Flash forward and I don't remember being discharged from the hospital or the ride to wherever we went, but I do remember falling again because my legs were still weak and not working properly. The time from waking up from my coma flashed one to the next with no memories between them. The best way to describe how I felt, it was like I was going in and out of consciousness but was awake to everyone around me. I was alert, or maybe seemed to be alert to those near me, but I wasn't. I remember being in a room with a man on his knees begging me to remember him. He said he was my husband, later I found out that was not true. I stood there frozen thinking "okay, you were just with Jesus. You remember seeing your daughter, two women, and now you're in this room." The house I was in was trashed and whoever decorated it had horrible taste in decor. I hated everything about it. I remember looking around, feeling like I needed to connect with just one item, but nothing I saw meant anything to me. I don't even remember walking into that room. It felt like I was in a Sci-Fi movie. I kept running through the memories I had, all 5 of them at this point. I felt like I was inside of someone else's body experiencing someone else's life. I saw the look of confusion and sadness on the man's face, and I wanted to lie, I wanted to make him feel better, but I couldn't. There was no way I was going to lie and make God think that my time with Jesus meant nothing to me. I knew I needed to hold on to being with Jesus if I was ever going to get back to him. I don't remember how I responded to him, but I didn't lie.

Chapter 15

The next thing I knew I was in a bedroom looking at clothes in a closet. This room was equally trashed, ransacked may be a better word to describe it honestly. Papers and clothes were tossed everywhere like someone was rummaging through my belongings looking for something of importance. Of course, when family and friends are told you have a 4% chance of living, people may think your belongings are fair game. I remember looking at all the clothes and nothing was familiar to me. I had gained weight when I was in my coma, something else I didn't know. What were they feeding me? Nonetheless, the clothes I had did not fit my body from being so swollen and nothing felt comfortable. I just wanted to lay down, close my eyes, and hear Jesus again. His voice was familiar and comforting, so I laid there restlessly and prayed. Suddenly there it was! I heard him loud and clear like a shout, "I said move!" It was Jesus and I finally felt okay. I remember jumping up, but my legs still didn't work, and my ears heard him clear as ever. He said it again, "move when I say move." His voice was calm, but strict and was the precise nudge that I needed to begin moving. I had made it to the top of the stairs when the man pushed me. I fell onto broken photos; someone had smashed all of them prior to my arrival back to this house. I ended up at the bottom of the steps, he was so angry that I couldn't remember him. I didn't know what I had done to make him this angry. I made it outside, but not before a fish tank came flying down on top of me. I heard the door slam shut and I remember crawling to the home next door. I prayed, "I hope this neighbor knows me!" The woman called 911 and sat there with me until the police came. I asked the woman, while we were waiting, if she knew who I was. She looked at me kind of confused. Can you imagine living next door and having your neighbor ask, "do you know who I am?" Apparently, I had lived there for a little while.

Chapter 16

My neighbor must have thought, "what is wrong with her?" or even "why is she asking me if I know who she is?" She did know me, and this wasn't hers, or my, first call to 911. The police coming and going from our home was an ongoing occurrence. When the police arrived, I was informed there was a no trespassing order filed against the man. How then, was this man even in my house? How was he there waiting for me? The police removed him from the property and began telling me all the steps I would need to take to keep myself safe. They also informed me of how he would show up at my home time and time again. There was even a missing child case and how they had to stop and come to and try to save me. I felt utterly horrible and beyond confused, but they did take the man away. I eventually went back into my house, but I did not know who to call. I am not sure about the amount of time that had passed before I heard from someone. I didn't know what to do, so I laid down and prayed. I remembered every moment of my time with Jesus in gratitude, tears were rolling down my face and I had such a longing to return to him. As time passed, I knew eventually someone was surely going to come and check on me. Sooner rather than later, I hoped. Eventually people started to come, and it was a lot to take in. Not only were they telling me who they were, but they were unknowingly telling me who I was. I was being told what I needed to do, and each seemed to know what was best for me. I was entirely lost and confused. I was sad. I kept thinking, "how was I just in the presence of Jesus and now I'm living in the middle of a tornado?" I felt like I was forever spinning with no point of touch down in sight, how could this all be happening?

Chapter 17

One memory that stands out for me is the feeling I had seeing my children walk through that door. I knew I needed my babies. I love them so much! They are beautiful, smart, and strong. They are the kind of women that would make any woman proud to be their mama. I also have a son-in-law, that apparently, I did not like prior to my coma. I truly don't understand why because he is the most wonderful man. I love him, and my babies, with all my heart. I knew being near my children felt right and it helped me. It helped me in more ways than I will ever be able to explain. I started to remember my children right away and it brought much needed comfort to me. My mother had traveled from Pennsylvania during my coma and continued to stay with me while I recovered. I was walking better, but my voice took a while longer to recover. All the tubes and breathing machine had strained my vocal cords. I remember listening to music for hours in my room. I identified with music on a deep level through the years. That was one of the things that I re-connected with almost immediately. I remembered my youth children too. Which was strange because they came during those 4-6 years of missing memories. I still hadn't regained those memories. Unfortunately, I did not get to pick and choose the memories that returned or stuck. I didn't like the look on people's faces when said I could remember one person and not another. Some were hurt, like I purposely chose to forget who they were, or they felt like they were less important to me. I was told that I needed to file an order for protection and go to court. I had not even slept once since I woke out of the coma. I was being ordered around to do this and must do that. I needed to file these protection orders before the man was released from jail. I didn't want to do anything. Not because I wanted this stranger back in my life around my children or myself, I didn't even know the man well enough to even miss him. At this point, I just wanted to lay down. I wanted to sleep. Having not slept since my coma, at this time days, made my body feel awful and like everything was continually on the go. All I wanted was to be back on that boat with Jesus. Nothing else mattered to me except getting back to Him. I felt like crawling into a dark place and disappearing. I was called a dummy and told I was not going to do anything. I didn't understand. I had multiple people telling me who I was, so many labels being placed on me, and it was overwhelming to say the least. I remember feeling like I just wanted to be left alone for a little while. I wanted the quiet and peace I had felt while I was with Jesus. I prayed to be back with Jesus. As I laid there praying, my youngest daughter brought her laptop into my room and said, "we love music, mama". That little girl can steal anyone's heart. She is such a beautiful blessing God has entrusted to me. We laid there next to each other listening to music for hours. We prayed and thanked Jesus for holding us together. She put on a song that I felt a deep connection to. "He Knows my Name" by McRaes. Even when I had no name, other than "November Female Unknown" He knew my name the entire time. He knew what I needed, and he knew me. "Something About That Name" came on next by Anne Wilson, then "Talking to Jesus" by Evolution Worship featuring Maverick City. All I could think was "I spoke with Jesus!" I stood there feeling his presence, I promise NOTHING and no one matter but getting to JESUS.

Chapter 18

How do you think you would feel if you were just face to face with Jesus? We laid there, worshiped, and praised God like never before. As tears rolled down my cheeks, I knew my identity was in Him. I mattered to him! I was enough for him! Now, fast forward a bit, if you were to talk with me today about Jesus you would know that nothing brings me to tears more than remembering his unconditional love and his voice. I knew my identity was in Christ. I knew that my next step, when made, would be because He told me to move and the next time, I paused it would be because He told me to stay. I knew I had to tune into His voice and remain there always. I knew listening to Him was the only way I was going to be okay. I knew that I had my children, and a youth group filled with young girls and boys, that were looking up to me. I knew that my next steps had to be ones of a Godly woman who is strong in her faith. I could not be that weak, broken woman who felt lost and fell back into that treacherous pattern. I was determined to be a mother, and youth leader, who put on the armor of God daily, always walking with Jesus. I knew in that moment who God was calling me to be. I wanted to be a woman of strength and a woman with dignity. I wanted to move forward with God, and I wanted to be whatever and wherever God told me to be. I've found my identity in Christ.

Chapter 19

As I began to grow differently in Christ, I wanted to teach them and even help mold them to move forward with grace. I wanted everything I did and do to reflect Jesus. So, I got up very early. At this point, I still hadn't slept, maybe only a cat nap here or there. Funny what being in a coma does to you. I whispered to my daughter "I am going to go make sure we are safe. I will be right back. I promise. You must stay here with grandma." and went out to my car. Everyone told me many did not think I would do what I needed too. Sitting in that car I knew I had to take my next step alone with Jesus. I did not need to post it on social media, and I didn't want the world to know. I didn't want a flood of people screaming or bashing a man that tried to kill me. I could have acted in multiple ways; I wanted my actions to reflect Jesus. I was not the woman I was before, whoever she was, but I knew that I wanted all of it to be over. I wanted my children and myself to be safe and to move forward with Jesus. I had to keep this man away from us and I needed to show my daughters that I would never again identify myself as a battered woman, but instead as a strong Godly woman. As I got into my car, although funny now, I thought "gosh, I sure hope I remember how to drive this thing." Depending on who you were to ask, I did. I sat in that car on that very early morning when the fog was still heavy in the air, and it just felt right. I must have spent a lot of time in that car singing because that's exactly what I did. As I drove to the courthouse, "Let me tell you about my Jesus" by Anne Wilson came on the radio. I was singing and dancing all the way there. When I arrived at the courthouse I called my baby sister; she always makes me feel braver than I really am. She told me "You got this!" and gave me one of her amazing sister pep talks. In that moment I felt like I could do what I needed to do. She always had my back. Love you, Sisser! I hung up and went into the courthouse to meet with a woman from domestic violence. How did I end up back here? Was abuse so deeply intertwined into my life that I seemed to seek it out? Why did I continue to deal with it since I was a small child? Was that a part of my identity I couldn't let go of? I sat there with that woman, explaining everything that had happened to me including being in a coma. I told her the stories that others had told me. I told her how I survived childhood abuse and domestic violence as an adult. I remembered that part of my past.

Chapter 20

I thought to myself "how did I end up with this back in my life?" "How did I allow this terribleness back in our lives?" That woman talked with me, she explained to me how women often go back, time and time again, and find familiarity in abuse. I left there thinking, and I was determined to never go back, and this was not going to be my story ever again. She told me about this missing girl named Gabby. She was all over the news, but I had no knowledge of who she was. I had not watched the news since waking up from my coma, but apparently this girl had gone missing, and a manhunt was underway. Everyone was looking for her and her boyfriend. I mention this because I will never forget, Gabby. I was able to get my order of protection immediately, which normally takes up to 72 hours to obtain. Can you imagine being scared for your life and being told you must wait 72 hours for an order to go into effect? In the meantime, the man who had done these terrible things to me had been released, and where did he go? Yep, right back to near where I was living. Like a shark circling its prey, he would circle my home wanting to talk with me. God kept me strong and kept telling me I needed to do this. That day those orders were filed, and the paperwork would be sent to all officers on duty. I got back home to and already busy house. Some of the people from church were there and my youth group children were there with my birth mom. They were cleaning the house for me and trying to get everything back in order. They brought plants and flowers. In the evening, my house would finally settle down when everyone went home. Alejandra, a sweet woman, that I had met through a Facebook bible study group stayed up with me for what may have seemed like days when we started messaging each other. Bless her. As I told her my story, she told me the God had plans for me and held my hand through those messages for a long time; and still does to this day. I've spoken with so many people over my days of recovery. I was awake for numerous days until the doctors finally gave me something to help me sleep. That man that hurt me was living a few doors down at this point. I could not leave my home by myself. I did not understand why he was still even hanging around when he had clearly moved on with someone else while I was in my coma. She was apparently a married woman, who later I came to understand, we had met the very day that I died. Why didn't he just stay gone? Why did he have to keep coming around? Did he feel the need to finish what he had started, and failed to accomplish? I had endless questions that I still have no answers for, but I was going to trust in God and his plans for me.

Chapter 21

I have concluded that I may never know why that man did not help me heal. Why was almost losing me in a coma not enough to change him? I mean, I didn't remember him at all. He had a clean slate chance to re-write our story. He could have been kind. He could have helped me recover from death. I was in an unfamiliar world, surrounded by unfamiliar people. I do not remember the man before my coma, but the man I do remember after it was not kind, nor gentle, whatsoever. I needed to move forward. I needed to focus on God's plan for me and I knew he has a reason for all that helped me. It helped me to not need to know all the answers to the questions that I had. I, we, must trust that his way is always better. His plans are always the best plans. I knew one thing for sure, I had spent time with Jesus! I heard His voice differently than many can ever relate to. I am thankful for my coma. That's a silly statement, isn't it? But that coma brought face to face with Jesus. You may want to think this was the end of the story for the guy who hurt me. I had the orders in place, that should have been enough, right? My son-in-law came and rebuilt my door frame that was kicked in by that man. He also did numerous other repairs of broken things. He secured doors and made sure he could not get in anywhere. All so we would feel safe. That man continued to come to our house every night. He took a tire off my car and another time took all the lug nuts except one off hoping I would drive down the road with unstable tires. He left flowers on my doorstep, then another time he sliced all my tires. After I had my protection order in place, he got sneakier. One night he waited outside in our backyard until I let my dog out. He jumped in through the back door, breaking our TV and throwing plants and dirt everywhere while saying things incoherently. He smelled strongly of alcohol. I showed him my phone and told him I had called 911 and they were in fact on their way. He did exactly what I prayed he would and ran off. Night after night he would come back and be gone before the police would come; it seemed like a never ending cycle. I begged the warrant officer and anyone else I encountered to please stop him. He would cause chaos then to hide at someone's home where the officers did not have the authority to go. I would tell everyone I knew that I had no trips planned and if I went missing to please search for me and to not let him hurt my girls. Praise God, he opened doors that no one else could and domestic violence was able to help relocate me and my family. I am thankful that they were able to relocate us well out of his reach. This all happened one day before his release yet again. Finally, we were going to have a new beginning, and a chance to start building our life in Christ. I prayed and still pray daily that he has spoken to Jesus about his past and that he has move forward, corrected his path, and that he too is now living for Jesus.

Chapter 22

Everyone I have told my story has had one comment at the end, "Everybody needs to hear your story!" I could not "go live" on Facebook. Remember from the beginning when I told you I am a big chicken when it comes to speaking in front of people? I knew I wanted to share what happened to me. I knew if I could share the story of my time with Jesus and express to everyone how loving and amazing he truly is maybe I could help just one person, or may lots of people, find their identity in Jesus. In this world I've felt lost, broken, and incomplete, but once I stood next to Him I knew NOTHING ELSE MATTERS except being sure that I will one day return to Him. So, if you have been one of the people who chose to sit and listen to the crazy coma lady and her raging rapids boat ride with Jesus, then I'm doing exactly what you said I should! I'm sharing my story the best way I know how; without standing in front of a room full of people. I've been called crazy multiple times in the past. Like when I would call somewhere, and they would ask me what the answer to my secret questions was or when I was asked to give my address and had no idea what it was. I turned and sank myself deep into the Bible. My older girls grew up with a pagan mom and lived a pagan lifestyle in the "blank days" as I call them. By the grace of God, I have found Jesus and turned away from paganism. I have fully given myself over to my Lord and Savior, Jesus Christ. I must make sure my youngest daughter knows the love of Jesus. I must be sure things are better and different for my youngest daughter. I haven't forgotten about the family image, but I am working on my identity in Christ and building myself in Him. There is a new song out that has helped me regain the memory from when I gave my life fully back to Jesus. Remember when I said I drove to a church in a truck and parked in the parking lot? I never owned that truck that I know of. But I was crying while sitting behind the steering wheel with a dashboard in front of me. I remember praying out loud and knowing I wanting to be in a church parking lot. I suppose I thought God would hear me better if I was closer to Him. FYI: God can hear you anywhere, even where you are sitting right now. Talk to Him, but if you feel the need to drive to a church parking lot then do that. He is worth the drive; I promise you that. While I was driving and listening to the radio the song "Windows Down" by Cain came on. I still do not have all my memory back, but from time to time I get a feeling or have a "foggy" memory. I'm told that one day all my memories may come back, but then again maybe they won't. Apparently, it's a form of amnesia or dementia both of which are related to the coma and covid. All I know is in that time I must have given my life back to Jesus. If I ever remember my "blank years", maybe I'll write about them too. As that song played on the radio, I felt that re-connection to Him, so to speak, and honestly it doesn't even matter when I gave my life back to him.

Chapter 23

God was the final one to give me the push I needed, to tell my story. I thought "okay, Lord. As soon as I hit the one year mark, I'll do it. I'm going to "go live" and tell everyone around the world about Jesus. It was going to be a big step for me, and I thought I could do it with only my youngest daughter and myself. I was excited to tell everyone about the time that I spent with Jesus. After all, how many truly get to say they have spoken with Jesus? I spoke with the pastor of the church, where I am a youth leader, and asked him "why did God send me back?" My thought to follow my question was "what if I don't make the boat next time?" I could feel that fear beginning to grow again with the "what ifs" that arose within me. Is it only me, or does that happen to you too? You take a step in faith, but then immediately step back due to fear and doubt. My head began to fill with thoughts of not being good enough and I could feel my doubts strengthening. Not once did my eyes drop from my Lord and Savior, but those old fears were starting to surface once again. I knew that I had to be sure I was working on

getting back to him one day at a time, and that nothing else mattered nearly as much in my life. I know that I need every person I meet to hear my story. I want to know with confidence that anytime I am around someone that they feel Jesus, just like I felt Jesus. I want everyone to know the importance of having Jesus at the center of their life and that nothing, past or present, matters. We all need to tune into His voice, so we know when he wants us to move or when we are to remain in place and wait. Who we are and what we do should always be done in His name.
As I spoke with my pastor, he told he that I'm still on that boat with Jesus and I need to start seeking my identity in Him. I know that my time with Jesus was real, and I must inform people of everything that he is.

Chapter 24

The Bible clearly states that men and women are created in God's image. All mankind was created to reflect God. Are you tuning into his voice? Are you in His word daily, and letting it guide you? Are you praying to Him for guidance, strength, and wisdom? Today when you we can literally identify as anything, as I said in the beginning of this book, so why not identify as God's child? Now let's continue, back to my huge one year mark. I gave myself all the pep talks I could come up with. I gave myself all the words of encouragement I could find. I knew I was ready; I was going to "go live" on Facebook. I laugh at the thought of being so stressed over such a silly little thing, but isn't that how Satan works? He gets into those little cracks of doubt and fear and opens them up into canyons. I kept telling myself "I'm going to tell everyone my story. I am going to be brave. I am going to do it!" Now, if you're a part of my "Facebook family" you have seen the big debut video of me chickening out. To tell you the truth, I refuse to allow myself to delete it. To this day, I still am nervous, awkward, and shy, but Jesus is still working in me. My youngest daughter and I spend our daily morning walks tuning into Our Lord together and put on our full armor of God.

If you have small children, I suggest trying this: Wake up in the morning and put on your full armor of God together. Talk about what it looks like and feels like. No answer they, or you, give is wrong. Some days my armor is heavy and dark. Other days it is bright and colorful. The armor fits the day, and no days are the same; just as no two people are the same. You will find your children excited to tell you about their armor each day and you'll be surprised how eager they are to hear about yours. It's such a wonderful way to remind our little ones to think of God daily and to let them know He is always with them. Giving your family a foundation in Christ is the best gift you will ever give them.

Just to help you out, here is what The Bible says:

New International Version (NIV)
The Armor of God

Ephesians 6:10-18

10 Finally, be strong in the Lord and in his mighty power. 11 Put on the full armor of God, so that you can take your stand against the devil's schemes. 12 For our struggle is not against flesh and blood, but against the rulers, against the authorities, against the powers of this dark world and against the spiritual forces of evil in the heavenly realms. 13 Therefore put on the full armor of God, so that when the day of evil comes, you may be able to stand your ground, and after you have done everything, to stand. 14 Stand firm then, with the belt of truth buckled around your waist, with the breastplate of righteousness in place, 15 and with your feet fitted with the readiness that comes from the gospel of peace. 16 In addition to all this, take up the shield of faith, with which you can

extinguish all the flaming arrows of the evil one. 17 Take the helmet of salvation and the sword of the Spirit, which is the word of God. 18 And pray in the Spirit on all occasions with all kinds of prayers and requests. With this in mind, be alert and always keep on praying for all the Lord's people.

Chapter 25

After my epic failure at my video, I dove deep into prayer and studying my Bible. I knew I needed to get my story out into the world, but I had no clue how I was going to do it. I messaged people. I stayed in constant prayer about it. I realized it was my story to tell and it was no one's responsibility to accomplish that task except mine. I refused to let Satan win. I knew if I was going to accomplish my goal of telling my story far and wide I had to continue to pray and seek my answer from God. This brings me to an amazing man, Jason David. I had the pleasure of meeting this man after my coma through social media. I came across him and his story while searching for my next bible teaching topic for my youth group. Jason was labeled with an identity he had no say in. He is so much more than "the cancer guy" and his beautiful wife is so much more than just a teacher. If you haven't heard of or read his story, you need to. I had linked up with this amazing couple for youth lessons to help cover my class while I was recovering. I had happened to see they were going on tour and would be close enough to drive to. I messaged them my story. I didn't expect a response, but they did response and with such love. They are God's people. We planned and met before their show as well as after. We chatted via messenger. After their show while I was chatting with his wife, Jason David said to me "I can't wait to read November Unknown." All I could think in that moment was "I have not written any of this down!" On my way home, I started writing this book. After all, it already had a name. Thank you, Jason, for the encouragement and letting God lead you. You have helped so many people, including myself. You see, I firmly believe that God places people in your life at the exact moment they need to be there. His timing is always perfect after all. It made me stop and think that maybe all the identities I once held had to be for me to be molded into the woman God wanted me to be today. In the end, none of it matters. What does matter is making sure Jesus knows my heart and through me I spread his message and love.

Chapter 26

I pray that if you knew me before my coma, as many people have, that you understand I am not the woman I was before my coma any longer I speak a little differently. My daughters know that I am different today and my son in law knows that I love him. My life is not perfect, please don't think that is what I am saying. I have great days and I have days that I fail. I even fall on my face from time to time, or even embarrass myself on social media. Above it all though, I will always put God first and I will always remain tuned into his voice. I will continue to grow in His love and seek him until I take my last breath in this life and once more am in His presence. I pray that if you are anywhere around me that you feel and see Jesus reflecting and shining through me. I pray that you find your identity in Him, because who you are in Christ is far more important than any other label or identity you will ever have. I identified with many Bible stories along my recovery journey.

Below are just a few.

Proverbs 31:25 She is clothed with strength and dignity. She laughs without fear of the future.

Matthew 18:3 Truly, I say to you, unless you turn and become like children, you will never enter the kingdom of heaven." If you are a follower of Jesus Christ, your core identity is that you are a child of God. "He predestined us to be adopted as sons through Jesus Christ for himself, according to the good pleasure of his will, to the praise of his glorious grace that he lavished on us in the Beloved One," writes Paul in Ephesians 1:5-6

Chapter 27

I could go on and on, quoting scripture that has helped me heal one after another. Scripture continues to heal us all as we continue our journey digging deep into The Bible. Once held the worst identities weather placed on me or I took on myself. I could have held on to those labels and that abused state of mind. But I have chosen to strip away those labels and let God's word fill my mind and heart. Hearing the voice of Jesus and feeling his presence standing so close to me was powerful. Who I was, what happened to me, my past mistakes, my failures, they no longer matter. I am forgiven. I am redeemed. Jesus died for me, and for you, so we could all be children of God. I know that I am the daughter of The King. I find my hopes, my dreams, my life, and who I am through Jesus Christ. No matter how dark your past is, no matter how big your mistakes those do not have to be your story. They can be a part of it, but they don't have to be all of it. If you put your full faith and trust in Jesus starting right now, today, he will be there for you. He will not run away or be angry with you.

Are you willing to take the first step? Are you willing to admit that you are a sinner, that Jesus gave his life for you, and are you willing to give your heart and soul over to Him fully? If so, read the prayer on the next page out loud. Or feel free to simply pray to God in your own words. Whether you're praying for yourself or someone else, just remember it doesn't have to be fancy. God knows your heart, after all He created you. So, when you are ready, turn the page, open your heart, and read the prayer.

Heavenly Father, I want to find my identity in you. I know a relationship with you will help me find it. I have been finding my identity in all the wrong places. Allowing the identity of others to fall on me, in all the wrong ways. I believe in Jesus, and I know that he died in my place. I know that he rose from the dead and lives. I trust that who I am in Him is far better than who I am in this world. I put my full trust and my full faith in Jesus Christ. Please forgive me for my sins through my faith in Him. I am and will be eternally in a relationship with you.

AMEN

You are free and you are clean. You have now been made a new, step forward and find your
identity in Christ. When he says move, now you move and when he says stay, you patiently stay. Tune into his voice, let Him guide you, and know it will all be okay.

Chapter 28

I am thankful for the foundation that was laid and the seeds that were planted when I was a little girl. The stories told by my grandparents and the lessons taught to me by a great youth pastor. Shout out to Mike, in Pennsylvania, the coolest youth pastor ever! In all honesty, if it wasn't for that foundation, and knowing where to run back to, I don't know if my story would be where I've been led to today. I am praying every day that my older daughters find Jesus too. That he has plans to place someone along their path, maybe even this story, that they see Jesus is the way and the truth. I pray that someone leads them to Christ. I am 100% okay with being identified as the praying mama and Nana or Mamaw: even the crazy Jesus lady. I don't care what comes my way because I know if I stay tuned into His voice and follow Him every moment of every day I will one day find my way back into His arms. Who knows, maybe we will even take another raging rapid boat ride.

P.S.

I felt the need to add just a bit more. I was going back through and proofreading all I've written, and started thinking maybe I should add this or change that. Overthinking everything like I tend to do and feeling that some of what I've said wasn't worded perfectly. So, as always, I took it to God through prayer. If I've learned anything reading the Bible, and growing in my relationship with God, is God wants us to pray. He wants to hear from us. I talk to Jesus all day, every day, he is my best friend. I started to pray for guidance, and for Him to show me what I need to keep and what I need to edit out. Have you ever prayed and got a completely different answer than you expected? Well, while I was praying, and considering taking this part out completely, the answer I was shown was to write in pen. What if more people would simply follow God's plan that he has written for us without doing our own edits? So, instead of a complete edit I chose to add a "P.S.", because I do not wish to alter what God has guided me to write in black and white. What I wanted to say was that my life might seems like it's been a traumatic and bad, but I've had great times, beautiful children, taken in children whom I've loved as my own, and met a plethora of amazing people through the years. I've also carried with me deep family roots of life, love, and values. I know now God has been with me in both my darkest and brightest moments. The identities I've spoken of in this book are the ones I've experienced during different stages in my life. I've written this book according to how I've viewed myself while growing up and what I've learned through the years.

After Thought

The only thing that matters in this life is your love for and getting back to Jesus, it's about finding who you are in him.

I just wanted to say, I may never know why you picked up this book. Maybe you don't know why you did either, but I'm sure thankful you did. Thank you for taking the time to read these pieces from my life. I pray this helped you. I pray God continues to use me to bring glory to his name forever until the day I'm back with him. I pray I get to meet you someday and I get to hear how this book turned your eyes towards Jesus and helped you to find who you are in him.

Help lines:

National Domestic Violence Hotline
Hours: 24/7. Languages: English, Spanish and 200+ through interpretation service
800-799-7233
SMS: Text START to 88788 988

Suicide and Crisis Lifeline
Hours: Available 24 hours
SMS: 988

National Center for Missing & Exploited Children's CyberTipline
Hours: 24-Hours Hotline 800-843-5678

Use the empty pages to inspire yourself or others. Begin writing your own story. Jot down your thoughts and prayers for the next 30 days. Write down what you feel you can't say to anyone. No matter what you choose to do with these empty pages, keep your eyes focused on moving when He says to move and staying only when Jesus says to stay. You'll be ok too;

Feel free to share your story with me on social media using **#IAMKNOWN** because the creator of the universe always knows you!